THE PILGRIMS

A BRIEF HISTORY FROM BEGINNING TO END

HISTORY ENCOUNTERS

Bonus Downloads

*Get Free Books with **Any Purchase**History Hub*

Every purchase comes with a FREE download!

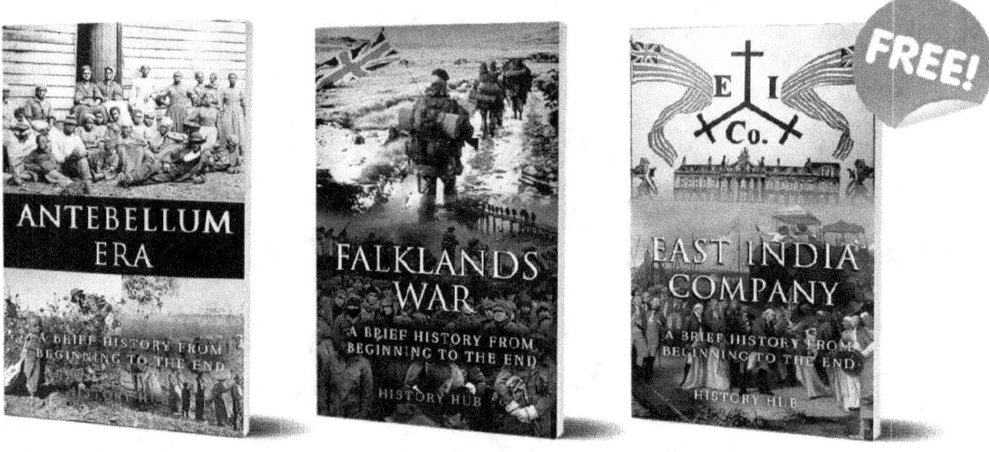

The Pilgrims

A Brief History from Beginning to the End

History Hub

CONTENTS

Chapter One
Introduction

Most people are familiar with the term "pilgrim," and yet, often, people aren't quite exactly sure who these people were or what historical relevance they hold. According to plimoth.org, "The people we know as Pilgrims have become so surrounded by legend that we are tempted to forget that they were real people." Pilgrims were, in fact, just regular English folk who, against all odds, set sail from England in 1620 on the Mayflower and landed on the shores of America. They then set about establishing their own colony in what would then become the state of Massachusetts. The Plymouth colony that would later be established by the Pilgrims would become the second British colony to be built on American soil.

The Pilgrims fled to the New World from England because of the government's suppression of their religious freedom. The

Pilgrims identified as Calvinist Protestants and worshiped God according to John Calvin's tenets.

In 1534, King Henry VIII, England's reigning monarch, broke away from the Roman Catholic Church. He chose to establish the Church of England, to which he was the head, not the Catholic Pope. In doing this, King Henry VIII set about changing the world as people knew it, including the lives of the Pilgrims. According to plimoth.org, "A few people felt that the new Church retained too many practices of the Roman Church. They called for a return to a simpler faith and less structured forms of worship. In short, they wanted to return to worship in the way the early Christians had. Because these people wanted to purify the church, they came to be known as 'Puritans.' Another group, considered very radical, went even further. They thought the new Church of England was beyond reform. Called 'Separatists,' they demanded the formation of new, separate church congregations. This opinion was very dangerous; in England in the 1600s, it was illegal to be part of any church other than the Church of England." In 1608, the Pilgrims petitioned the King for permission to establish their own religious community and were turned down; they sought another place to live. The Pilgrims wanted to be able to worship God in whichever way they saw fit, so they decided to relocate to Holland, a country known for its tolerance of all faiths. However, the Pilgrims soon saw that life in Holland had a negative impact on their children, so they left the country just twelve years later, in 1620. They returned to England, but they knew they could not stay and live the life they wanted to, so they remained only long enough to prepare for their voyage to the New World.

To make the great voyage to the New World, the first Pilgrims (or Puritans as they were then known) would have to travel across the great Atlantic, and they did so on none other than a ship named the Mayflower. They anchored their boat at Plymouth Rock on 11 December 1620 and made haste for landfall. What faced them was an unknown world, a new world in which they would indelibly leave their mark in a myriad of different ways.

In order to truly know who the Pilgrims were and their historical importance, we must know more about their incredible journey and go beyond the myth surrounding them.

Chapter Two
The Origins of the Pilgrims

The Early Days in England

The Pilgrims' tale began in the remote English county of Nottinghamshire and Yorkshire. A tiny group of Church of England believers gathered there. These individuals believed that the Church of England had strayed and was no longer properly worshiping God. They believed that the New Church formed by King Henry VIII still had too many Roman Catholic influences, which they did not like. They also found the Church of England to be too corrupt to be capable of reform. Although they would later earn the title of the Pilgrims, this group of individuals was known as the Puritans. The Puritans desired to establish a completely new, pure church. According to billofrightsinstitute.org, "over the years, pressure had been mounting on organizations like the Puritans, and the English government saw these religious dissenters as a threat to the fabric of English society." The Puritan meetings came to the attention of the Bishop of York in 1607, who then started to take action against them and many of the individuals feared for their lives. The congregation soon understood that practicing their faith in England was no longer possible. For one that offered at least the possibility of freedom, they had to leave the world they were familiar with.

The congregation made the difficult decision to emigrate to Holland. According to billofrightsinstitute.org, "Most rural peoples never traveled more than a few miles from their home in their lifetimes. The world beyond their villages and counties was utterly foreign to them. Additionally, the English government would not allow anyone to leave without permission. The congregation fled in secrecy."

The Move to Holland

The Puritans arrived in Holland filled with hope that this could become their new homeland, a place where they could practice religious freedom in peace and out from under the oppressive thumb of the New Church of England. When they arrived in Holland, the Puritans were initially hesitant, faced with a strange new place that was quite unlike their home villages, not only in terms of size but also in terms of culture. Yet despite this apprehension, they did their best to fit in and make the best of their new location. The Puritans made their home in the tens of thousands-strong city of Leiden. The fast-paced commercial city was a stark contrast to the English farmers' upbringing of seasonal, slow-paced life. The Pilgrims didn't take long to start feeling alienated from the agricultural English ideals and heritage they valued due to the city's culture and character. They began to feel that their children would fall prey to the wrong influences. Life was also harder than they'd anticipated. William Bradford, who was one of the Puritans who sailed on the Mayflower in 1620, noted the following about his time in Holland and that of his fellow congregation:

For these & other reasons they removed to Leyden, a fair &bewtifullcitie, and of a sweete situation, but made more famous by ye universitiewherwith it is adorned, in which of late had been so many learned man. But wanting that traffike by sea which Amerstdaminjoyes, it was not so beneficiall for their outward means of living &estats. But being now hear pitchet they fell to such trads &imployments as they best could; valewing peace & their spirituallcomforte above any other riches whatsoever. And at length they came to raise a competente&comforteable living, but with hard and continuall labor.

Exit From Holland

In addition to their hardships, the Puritans also came to understand that they were not as far from England's reach as they had thought. They were still being monitored by the Dutch government, and again, they began to feel unsafe. They were careful about who they met in public and what they said to others in situations where they might be overheard by an English or Dutch spy. Only a few years after arriving in Holland, the Puritans decided that they must go somewhere else, far from Europe, if they truly wished to experience religious freedom. According to Bradford, they wished to find "a better and easier place of living" where their children would be safe from "evil examples into extravagance and dangerous courses" and a home for them all where they could have "great hope, for the propagating and advancing the gospel of the kingdom of Christ in those remote parts of the world."

So now they were faced with a myriad of questions and uncertainty about the future, "Where could they go and still maintain their heritage and lifestyle?" The persistence and prevalent "religious and political unrest on the continent of

Europe meant moving further inland was not an option," so the Puritans decided to look elsewhere, and they turned their eyes west "to a new and unknown world."

Chapter Three
Leaving Europe

Where to Next?

The Puritans knew that they needed to leave Europe; however, they were unsure as to where to go next. According to Edward Winslow, another Puritan who traveled on the Mayflower to the New World in 1620, it was very important for the congregation to "retain their English identity, culture and language" wherever they went next.

There were so many variables that they must take into consideration. As the billofrightsinstitute.org details, they would first "need permission from the English crown to settle on the lands there. Next, they would need to finance the expedition and find a ship and a crew willing to make the dangerous and long journey. They needed to buy enough supplies to get them across the ever turbulent north Atlantic and then have enough to settle in the new continent. They knew almost nothing of the area they were traveling to. Unknown American Indians, animals, and weather all awaited them on the new shore."

The decision to immigrate to a country like America was fraught with uncertainty at the time due to reports of failed colonies. There were worries that the locals would be hostile, that there wouldn't be any food or water, that they may come into contact with unidentified diseases, and that traveling by sea was always dangerous. However, they felt pressured for a time as the truce that had been struck after the Eighty Years' War was in jeopardy, and there was anxiety among the congregation at how this might again change the tides in Europe.

There were a few locations that the Puritans considered. One possible location was Guiana, where the Dutch had founded the Essequibo colony on the northeastern coast of

South America. Another option was the Virginia colonies which had settled in America in 1907. Virginia was a desirable location because the older colony there may provide better security and trade opportunities, but they also had to be careful to avoid settling too close since doing so might unintentionally recreate the political climate back in England.

According to Bradford, in the end, the chosen settlement site was at the mouth of the Hudson River. The London Company governed a sizable tract in the area. There were also military and economic advantages of being adjacent to an existing colony that was still guaranteed, allaying their concerns about social, political, and religious disputes. It was two Puritan leaders, John Carver and Robert Cushman, who traveled to England in order to acquire a land patent which they were able to acquire in June 1619. According to billofrightsinstitute.org, "After much diligence, the congregation eventually secured a patent in 1619 from the Virginia Company, a private joint-stock venture which technically owned the land in North America. This patent would allow them to settle in North America while retaining a sense of their English identity."

The land patent was awarded on one condition, and that was made by the King, and that was that the "Leiden group's religion would not receive official recognition." Despite having secured the land patent, the Leiden group ran into several issues that delayed them for months before they could finally begin to make proper preparations. Not every member of the congregation could leave on the initial journey to the New World due to several reasons, including budget constraints. The group determined that the initial settlement should be handled mostly by younger and stronger members and the rest of the congregation promised to follow when and if they could. A senior elder and the leader of the congregation, Willian Brewster, was assigned to oversee the American congregation, while Pastor John Robinson would stay in Leiden with the majority of the church. Although it was decided that the church in America would be operated independently, it was also decided that people who migrated between the two congregations would automatically become members of both.

Once they had settled their personal and professional affairs, the first group of Puritans, who would soon become the Pilgrims, acquired supplies and a small ship called the Speedwell. According to Bradford, the Speedwell would be used to "bring some passengers from the Netherlands to England, then on to America where it would be kept for the fishing business, with a crew hired for support services during the first year." They had also leased a large ship called the Mayflower that would be used for transport and exploration. These ships were described as "small, cramped vessels that leaked in heavy seas and lacked any comforts for onboard passengers."

Chapter Four
The Voyage to the New World

A Tearful Farewell to Europe

There are several accounts made by those passengers who left for the New World and how challenging it was for them to part from their family and friends. No one knew quite what awaited them across the Atlantic, and there were many risks. Whether they would ever see them again, no one could say for certain.

These accounts came from individuals such as leader Edward Winslow who said that at the ships' departure:

> *A flood of tears was poured out. Those not sailing accompanied us to the ship, but were not able to speak to one another for the abundance of sorrow before parting.*

Bradford also described the departure of the first batch of Pilgrims:

Truly doleful was the sight of that sad and mournful parting. To see what sighs and sobs and prayers did sound among them; what tears did gush from every eye, and pithy speeches pierced each heart...their Reverend Pastor, falling down on his knees, and they all with him...

The initial journey took three days on a ship called the Speedwell. The group traveled down the south coast of England and arrived at Southampton on 5 August 1620. It was here that the Pilgrims first saw the Mayflower, which was being loaded with the supplies and provisions they would need not only on their journey but once they arrived in the New World. Together the two ships set sail for America, blissfully unaware that they were about to happen upon some stormy seas.

A Sinking Speedwell

After meeting up with the Mayflower, the two ships set off from America. However, soon after this, the Speedwell crew reported that their ship was taking on water. The crew managed to seal the leaks and continued. However, more than 200 miles past Land's End on the southwest coast of England, the ship sprung a third leak, and this time, they had no alternative but to leave Speedwell behind. According to billofrightsinstitute.org, "The Speedwell began leaking so badly that the Pilgrims decided they needed to return to England. It was now mid-August, and the Pilgrims began facing the daunting prospect of a fall crossing and winter landing in the New World." Eventually, they came to the decision to leave the Speedwell behind as they could not waste any more time." This was a difficult decision, and it had tragic consequences as both critical resources had to be left behind as there was not enough space on the Mayflower alone. Some twenty Speedwell passengers joined the now-crowded Mayflower, and those passengers who could not fit onto the Mayflower were forced to return to Holland to await the next trip.

After the loss of the Speedwell, there was a general air of disappointment among the Pilgrims, most of whom were keen to set sail. However, the winds were not in their favor, and for over a week, the Mayflower sat. Bradford was particularly concerned about the situation. In his notes, he writes:

We lie here waiting for as fair a wind as can blow... Our victuals will be half eaten up, I think, before we go from the coast of England; and, if our voyage last long, we shall not have a month's victuals when we come in the country.

In addition to being anxious to set sail, Bradford was also suspicious of the Speedwell's seaworthiness which he noted had "made many voyages... to the great profit of her owners." He found it strange that she had suddenly fallen prey to so many leaks, which he believed were the fault of the Master, who employed "cunning and deceit" in order to stop their voyage at the fear of finding starvation, disease, and death in the New World.

Take to the Seas

On 6 September 1620, they finally sailed out for sea once more, packing the Mayflower with as many passengers and supplies as they dared. The crew and passengers sighed with relief to finally be on their way, and yet they had a long journey ahead of them, one that would test their faith, determination, and patience.

Despite its pretty name, the Mayflower was uncomfortable, stuffy, and damp, and as the days passed by, the atmosphere grew dismal. The ship made its way slowly across the North Atlantic for sixty-five days. The Mayflower was pounded by ferocious gales and heavy seas on their journey. The passengers and crew were constantly damp and shivering from the ocean spray that seeped through the ship's seams. They experienced seasickness, cold, and frustration from being cooped up with the same people day after day without a break. It was a journey that tested them all and one that seemed as if it would never end.

Chapter Five
The New World

Arrival

On 6 November 1620, the Mayflower finally caught its first glimpse of the New World. However, what they saw was not the Hudson River; rather, they realized that their route had left them much farther north, off the Cape Cod coast. This was where their real challenge started. They were left with nothing but their wits and their supplies to keep them alive when they found themselves off the coast of an uncharted and frigid shoreline.

Mutiny on Board the Mayflower

Tensions among the colonists surfaced even before they disembarked the Mayflower because it had landed in Massachusetts instead of Virginia. Those not part of the congregation claimed the contract with the Virginia Company was null and void. They believed they were free of the charter's jurisdiction because the Mayflower had landed in disputed waters.

Because they had no central authority, the hostile outsiders flatly refused to follow any established norms. William Bradford, the leader of the Pilgrims, later stated that "several strangers made discontented and mutinous speeches." They knew they needed to do something before all hell broke loose on the ship.

The Mayflower Compact

The passengers aboard the Mayflower came together to "form a covenant with God and each other." Called the Mayflower Compact, this was the Pilgrims founding political document. According to histroy.com, "While still on board the ship, a group of 41 men signed the so-called Mayflower Compact, in which they agreed to join together in a 'civil body politic.' This document would become the foundation of the new colony's government. Signed on November 11, 1620, the Mayflower Compact was the first document to establish self-government in the New World."

Here is the full Mayflower Compact:

In the name of God, Amen. We, whose names are underwritten, the Loyal Subjects of our dread Sovereign Lord King James, by the Grace of God, of Great Britain, France, and Ireland, King, defender of the Faith, etc.:

Having undertaken, for the Glory of God, and advancements of the Christian faith, and the honor of our King and Country, a voyage to plant the first colony in the Northern parts of Virginia; do by these presents, solemnly and mutually, in the presence of God, and one another; covenant and combine ourselves together into a civil body politic; for our better ordering, and preservation and furtherance of the ends aforesaid; and by virtue hereof to enact, constitute, and frame, such just and equal laws, ordinances, acts, constitutions, and offices, from time to time, as shall be thought most meet and convenient for the general good of the colony; unto which we promise all due submission and obedience.

In witness whereof, we have hereunto subscribed our names at Cape Cod the 11th of November, in the year of the reign of our Sovereign Lord King James, of England, France, and Ireland, the eighteenth, and of Scotland the fifty-fourth, 1620.

In layman's terms, the compact outlined the following rules for the self-governed New World:

- Despite their desire for independence; the colonists would remain faithful subjects of King James.

- For the benefit of the colony, the settlers agreed to draft and implement "laws, ordinances, acts, constitutions, and offices..."

- It was agreed that the colonists would unite under a single society and work together to advance that society.

- the colonists would practice their Christian beliefs in their daily lives.

Chapter Six
Settling in Plymouth

The Mayflower eventually settled in what would become known as Plymouth Harbor, situated on the west side of Cape Cod Bay in the middle of December.

An initial group of passengers had been sent out from the Mayflower to explore the new territory in search of potential dangers of potential problems. Their small shallop had been damaged on the voyage, and so the passengers went to the beach on foot to collect firewood and to take long-awaited (albeit rather chilly) baths in the ocean. The colonists relied heavily on the Mayflower as a floating home for the first few months.

In Bradford's book Of Plymouth Plantation, he makes a record of some of their earlier experiences when the men went on foot to explore the surrounding area. He notes how they encountered an Indian grave which was decorated in corn. The colonists took the corn, hoping to plant it as their first crop. Bradford notes:

They also found two of the Indian's houses covered with mats, and some of their implements in them; but the people had run away and could not be seen. Without permission they took more corn, and beans of various colours. These they brought away, intending to give them full satisfaction (payment) when they should meet with any of them, – as about six months afterwards they did.

And it is to be noted as a special providence of God, and a great mercy to this poor people, that they thus got seed to plant corn the next year, or they might have starved; for they had none, nor any likelihood of getting any, till too late for the planting season.

After the shallop was repaired, the colonists made frequent trips to shore via shallop to lay the groundwork for their new store and residential structures.

According to Verlyn Klinkenborg, author of *Why Was Life So Hard for the Pilgrims?*, "By December, most of the passengers and crew had become ill, coughing violently. Many were also suffering from the effects of scurvy. There had already been ice and snowfall, hampering exploration efforts; half of them died during the first winter."

History.com notes that during this first winter, "leaders such as Bradford, Standish, John Carver, William Brewster, and Edward Winslow played important roles in keeping the remaining settlers together. In April 1621, after the death of the settlement's first governor, John Carver, Bradford was unanimously chosen to hold that position; he would be reelected 30 times and served as governor of Plymouth for all but five years until 1656."

Interestingly the term pilgrim was first ever recorded by Bradford in his book *Of Plymouth Plantation*. When he talked about the departure in July 1620 from Holland, he referred to the Hebrews in the Old Testament as "strangers and pilgrims" who were given the chance to go back to their old country but who chose instead to go forth and search for a better, heavenly country. His account is as follows:

> *So they lefte [that] goodly &pleasantecitie, which had been ther resting place, nere 12 years; but they knew they were pilgrimes, & looked not much on these things; but lift up their eyes to ye heavens, their dearest cuntrie, and quieted their spirits.*

Are You Enjoying Reading?

As an independent publisher

with a tiny marketing budget

we rely on readers, like you.

If you're receiving help from this book,

would you please take a moment to write a brief review?

We really appreciate it.

Chapter Seven
The Wampanoag People and the First Thanksgiving

The Wampanoag People

More than four months after their arrival, the colonists finally met and interacted with the Wampanoag tribe, despite having caught glimpses of them on occasion the two communities had not come into contact. By March of 1621, they had negotiated a pact of mutual protection with Ousamequin, chief of the neighboring Pokanoket Wampanoag tribe (also known as Massasoit to the Pilgrims). There were six stipulations to the agreement. No one would do anything to hurt the other. Everything that was stolen would be given back, and the thief would be sent back to his own people to face justice. When the two groups got together, they made a pact to leave their weapons behind and work together as allies during battle. A

Wampanoag by the name of Squanto could speak English. He had previously been captured by British sailors and had been living in London. He joined the colonists and taught them how to cultivate Indian maize.

The First Thanksgiving

The first American Thanksgiving was celebrated between the Pilgrims and a tribe of Native Americans known as the Wampanoag. There are several accounts of what occurred. According to history.com, the first American thanksgiving holiday "dates back to November 1621, when the newly arrived Pilgrims and the Wampanoag Indians gathered at Plymouth for an autumn harvest celebration." Britannica notes that "in the fall of 1621, the harvest was good. To celebrate, the roughly 50 surviving Pilgrims held a feast. In addition to harvested grains and vegetables, they prepared seafood and fowl—ducks, geese, and possibly turkey. They were probably surprised when a group of about 90 Wampanoag arrived. But the Wampanoag offered to share their deer meat, and the groups spent time together peacefully for three days. This event became known as the first Thanksgiving."

Winslow wrote about the experience as noted below:

"Our corn did prove well, and God be praised, we had a good increase of Indian corn, and our barley indifferent good, but our peas not worth gathering, for we feared they were too late sown. They came up very well, and blossomed, but the sun parched them in the blossom. Our harvest being gotten in, our governor sent four men on fowling, that so we might after a special manner rejoice together, after we had gathered the fruits of our labors; they four in one day killed as much fowl, as with a little help beside, served the company almost a week, at which time amongst other recreations, we exercised our arms, many of the Indians coming amongst us, and amongst

the rest their greatest king Massasoit, with some ninety men, whom for three days we entertained and feasted, and they went out and killed five deer, which they brought to the plantation and bestowed on our Governor, and upon the Captain and others. And although it be not always so plentiful, as it was at this time with us, yet by the goodness of God, we are so far from want, that we often wish you partakers of our plenty."

What Did They Eat?

In 1621, the Pilgrims celebrated their first autumn harvest, and it's likely that they dined on the fruits of their labor with the assistance of their Wampanoag neighbors. Onions, beans, lettuce, spinach, cabbage, carrots, and maybe even peas are just some of the local veggies that would have been served. In addition, corn, which historical records suggest was abundant during the first harvest, may have been provided, albeit likely not in the form most modern diners are accustomed to. The corn would have been shelled and ground into cornmeal, then boiled and mashed into a thick corn mush or porridge, often sweetened with molasses.

Whether they had turkey for their thanksgiving feast is debatable. In On Plymouth Plantation, Bradford noted that the colonists had a bountiful fall harvest because "there was great store of wild turkeys, of which they took many, besides venison." Indeed, both English settlers and Native Americans relied heavily on wild turkey (but not domesticated turkey) as a food supply. Nonetheless, it is also possible that the hunters brought back other birds like ducks, geese, and swans, which we know the colonists ate on a regular basis. Herbs, onions, or nuts might have been used to enhance the flavor of the birds in place of bread stuffing.

Chapter Eight
Thanksgiving

The Thanksgiving Myth

It is largely agreed that the first Thanksgiving was peaceful. However, in the last fifty years, the origins of Thanksgiving have become quite controversial among scholars to the point that many have dedicated their careers to debunking the "Thanksgiving Myth," as they call it.

According to author David Silverman who wrote *This Land Is Their Land: The Wampanoag Indians, Plymouth Colony, and the Troubled History of Thanksgiving*, the Thanksgiving Myth "is that friendly Indians, unidentified by tribe, welcome the Pilgrims to America, teach them how to live in this new place, sit down to dinner with them and then disappear. They handed off America to white people so they could create a great nation dedicated to liberty, opportunity, and Christianity for the rest of the world to profit from. That's the story—it's about Native people conceding to colonialism. It's bloodless and in many ways an extension of the ideology of Manifest Destiny."

Furthermore, the thanksgiving myth assumes that the Native people willingly gave America to the colonizers when this is not the case. They were happy and had a great life before the Pilgrims arrived. Of course, the Wampanoag story is not one as popular as that of the Pilgrims, but it still deserves to be told. The Wampanoag, also known as the "People of the First Light," were excellent custodians of the land and seas around their territory because they had lived there for almost 12,000 years. They were able to create a favorable environment for themselves and other forms of life by controlling the resources available in their environment. Planting for maximum harvests while keeping pests at bay was second nature to them, and they knew how to care for the soils that gave life to maize, beans, and squash, as well as other squashes like pumpkins and zucchini.

The meat of a variety of animals, including deer, moose, beaver, raccoon, and others, supplemented their diets. Because they were a frugal people, the Wampanoag made use of every component of the animals they killed and carried home, including the skins, bones, and teeth. They lived a free and peaceful life until the colonists arrived and changed everything. The Pilgrims are often seen as the "heroes" of the thanksgiving story when in fact, there were no heroes. They did not bring the Native people anything that made them "better off."

Another failure of history when it comes to the thanksgiving story, as Silverman wrote, is that people assume that "history doesn't begin for Native people until Europeans arrive. People had been in the Americas for at least 12,000 years and, according to some Native traditions, since the beginning of time. And having history start with the English is a way of dismissing all that. The second is that the arrival of the Mayflower is some kind of first-contact episode. It's not.

Wampanoags had a century of contact with Europeans–it was bloody, and it involved slave raiding by Europeans. At least two and maybe more Wampanoags, when the Pilgrims arrived, spoke English, had already been to Europe and back, and knew the very organizers of the Pilgrims' venture."

The Wampanoag and Pilgrims After 1621

The Wampanoag tribe helped the Pilgrims because they believed the relationship would be mutually beneficial. Before their arrival, the Wampanoags had been devastated by a disease, which greatly diminished their population. So, the Wampanoag made peace with the Pilgrims, but it wasn't because they wanted to do it. As noted on the website mayflower400.org, "This 'peace' was not necessarily one the Wampanoag were comfortable with. For a period, the two groups' interests aligned – but in the context of 400 years of history, it is a moment in time."

They hoped to work with the Pilgrims but after their thanksgiving meal. The relationship became strained. Of course, it did not help that their translator, Squanto, perished in 1622 while guiding Bradford's Cape Cod voyage.

The more Pilgrims who arrived, the worse the relations crumbled, and tempers flared. The invaders introduced new diseases to which the indigenous people of the Americas had no defenses. The spread of smallpox would decimate populations still rebuilding after the Great Death. There was an upsurge in violent acts.

The Wampanoag, who had maintained a harmonious relationship with the natural world for generations, found themselves in the minority in their own territories by the 1630s, despite having maintained a proud and environmentally conscious way of life for millennia. The first missionaries to visit the Wampanoag area landed in 1632. A man named John Eliot traveled all the way from Cambridge, England, in an effort to convert the Wampanoag to Christianity by translating the Bible and other Christian texts into Wopanaak (the Wampanoag language).

Still, war was on the horizon. The Pequot War, which began in 1637 as a result of European colonization of Massachusetts Bay and New England, resulted in the ruthless eradication of the Pequot people. There was going to be more fighting.

Massasoit's collaboration with the Pilgrims threw off the balance of power among the local Native American communities. This was especially true of the Massachusetts and Narragansett tribes, who did not look favorably on the arrival of European settlers. Relations between settlers and Native Americans worsened during the succeeding decades as the former group expanded its territorial holdings. Before his death in 1657, William Bradford had voiced concern that violence might soon rip New England apart.

After his father's death in 1662, Metacomet, Ousamequin's son and heir, became convinced that the colonists were no longer honoring the relationship his father had formed.

Furthermore, the colonists were constantly encroaching against Wampanoag territory. The atmosphere between the two sides became hostile. The colonists insisted that the Wampanoag turn over all of their weapons as part of the peace treaty and executed three members of the tribe in 1675 for the slaying of Christian local John Sassamon, who had warned the Plymouth Colony of an impending attack on English colonies.

King Philip, a name given to Metacomet by the English, led a rebellion of the Wampanoag, Nipmuck, Pocumtuck, and Narragansett peoples. The largest army the colonial leaders could organize, fighting in alliance with other tribes, was what they faced. The 14-month conflict is widely regarded as a desperate attempt to expel the colonists. In terms of American casualties, it ranks as the bloodiest conflict in our nation's history.

According to conneticuthistory.org, "King Philip's War has been called United States' most devastating conflict. One in 10 soldiers on both sides was killed, 1,200 colonists' homes were burned, and vast stores of foodstuffs were destroyed. The effects of the carnage and property damage were felt for years by colonists. The war's ramifications for Native populations of southern New England included not only loss of life and, for some, enslavement but the continued erosion of sovereignty, land rights, and communities as well."

Chapter Nine
The Pilgrim Legacy

Governance

Bradford became governor after Carver's death in 1621. Many times reelected, he presided over Plymouth's development for the next 35 years. Bradford and other religious leaders ruled the colony and established democratic institutions like voting and town meetings.

New Arrivals

More English colonists arrived during the next six years, and those left behind in England or Holland when the Mayflower sailed were eventually able to join their families in the New World. Many people in England at the time of the Pilgrims left because of religious persecution at the hands of King James I and his successor, Charles I. After the Mayflower's arrival, three other ships, the Fortune, the Anne, and the Little James, made their way to Plymouth (both 1623). Their charter from King Charles I stated that Governor John Winthrop and a party of about a thousand Puritan refugees settled in Massachusetts in 1630. Winthrop quickly made Boston the seat of government for the Massachusetts Bay Colony, which would go on to become the region's most populated and successful colony. Plymouth Colony had established a secure lifestyle by 1627. The harvests were plentiful, and families expanded. Plymouth Colony had a population of roughly 160 in 1627.

Trade, Industry, and Progress

The colony's progress toward success was gradual. Colonists farmed land, kept livestock, and bartered with indigenous people. They shipped furs and timber back to England. They repaid the London firm that had funded their journey in 1627. In the years following 1630, Plymouth grew richer thanks to trade with the nearby Puritan colony of Massachusetts Bay Colony. There was a mass exodus of Plymouth colonists to farms and ranches outside of the city. According to history.com, 'compared with later groups who founded colonies in New England, such as the Puritans, the Pilgrims of Plymouth failed to achieve lasting economic success. After the early 1630s, some prominent members of the original group, including Brewster, Winslow, and Standish, left the colony to build their own communities. The cost of fighting King Philip's War further damaged the colony's struggling economy. Less than a decade after the war, King James II appointed a colonial governor to rule over New England, and in 1692, Plymouth was absorbed into the larger entity of Massachusetts.

The Pilgrims Today

The modern-day view of the Pilgrims is vastly different from a hundred years ago. According to the University of California, "by 1970, the cultural tide had turned. Representatives of the Wampanoag nation walked out of Plymouth's public celebration of Thanksgiving that year to announce that the fourth Thursday in November should instead be known as the National Day of Mourning. To these protesters, 1620 represented violent conquest and dispossession, the twinned legacies of exclusion."

Previously, the Pilgrim story had been a single narrative, one that had been told and retold for more than two centuries. Yet people wanted a "historically accurate and culturally inclusive history."

In their own right, the Pilgrims were brave, and they took a step out of their comfort zone in search of the life they truly wanted. Yet, like the story of all colonizers in the modern day, they will always be the villains of one narrative.

Chapter Ten
Conclusion

In today's society, the term pilgrim has come to mean something different than it did five hundred years ago. In today's terms, we often think of a pilgrim as a traveler who goes to an exotic location, usually for spiritual purposes. A pilgrimage is a common phrase used now when someone goes in search of themselves or some greater meaning. Yet the central message and goals of the 1620's Pilgrims are something that very much still exists in society today.

Astronaut Buzz Aldrin once said that "the pilgrims on the Mayflower landed at Plymouth Rock. To my knowledge, they didn't wait around for a return trip to Europe. You settle someplace with a purpose. If you don't want to do that, stay home. You avoid an awful lot of risks by not venturing outward." What Aldrin says is both relevant and poignant. The

Pilgrims took risks for what they believed in and the lives they wished to live. They took their young families on a dangerous journey to a land that they did not know, and yet they did so in search of a better life, a life of fulfillment and purpose.

Perhaps if we can learn anything from the Pilgrims' story, it is how to take risks and venture outward, even in the face of uncertainty. If we can go as far as to compare the Pilgrims to modern-day astronauts, then venturing to the New World was equally as great a journey as traveling to the moon.

According to billofrightsinstitute.org, "The Pilgrims' decision to settle in North America created immense challenges. First, they would need permission from the English crown to settle on the lands there. Next, they would need to finance the expedition and find a ship and a crew willing to make the dangerous and long journey. They needed to buy enough supplies to get them across the ever turbulent north Atlantic and then have enough to settle in the new continent. They knew almost nothing of the area they were traveling to. Unknown American Indians, animals, and weather all awaited them on the new shore."

The Pilgrims believed in their journey; this belief is, without a doubt, something to admire. Yet, like the story of all explorers of the New World, it is more complicated than it appears. When the Pilgrims arrived on the shores of America, it was already occupied by the native people who saw the land as their own and had established roots there. Yet, as is the case around the world, the Pilgrims and the Native Americans tried to live together, but in the end, peace was overthrown by bloodshed.

Chapter Eleven
Discussion Question

Most people are familiar with the term "Pilgrim," and yet, often, people aren't quite exactly sure who these people were or what historical relevance they hold. According to plimoth.org, "The people we know as Pilgrims have become so surrounded by legend that we are tempted to forget that they were real people." Before reading the above discussion on the Pilgrims, what did you know about them? What is the most important thing you've learned about them now? Discuss.

Discussion Question

The congregation made the difficult decision to emigrate to Holland. According to billofrightsinstitute.org, "most rural peoples never traveled more than a few miles from their home in their lifetimes. The world beyond their villages and counties was utterly foreign to them. Additionally, the English government would not allow anyone to leave without permission. The congregation fled in secrecy." What does this say about the power and influence of religion?

Discussion Question

The Puritans knew that they needed to leave Europe; however, they were unsure as to where to go next. According to Edward Winslow, another Puritan who traveled on the Mayflower to the New World in 1620, it was very important for the congregation to "retain their English identity, culture, and language" wherever they went next." Why do you think it was important for the Puritans to retain their identity, culture, and language? Discuss.

Discussion Question

The Thanksgiving Myth says "that friendly Indians, unidentified by tribe, welcome the Pilgrims to America, teach them how to live in this new place, sit down to dinner with them and then disappear. They handed off America to white people so they could create a great nation dedicated to liberty, opportunity, and Christianity for the rest of the world to profit from. That's the story—it's about Native people conceding to colonialism. It's bloodless and in many ways an extension of the ideology of Manifest Destiny." Has your perception of Thanksgiving changed now that you know about the myth? Why or why not? Discuss.

Discussion Question

Despite its pretty name, the Mayflower was uncomfortable, stuffy, and damp, and as the days passed by, the atmosphere grew dismal. The ship made its way slowly across the North Atlantic for sixty-five days. The Mayflower was pounded by ferocious gales and heavy seas on their journey. The passengers and crew were constantly damp and shivering from the ocean spray that seeped through the ship's seams. They experienced seasickness, cold, and frustration from being cooped up with the same people day after day without a break. It was a journey that tested them all and seemed like it would never end. How do you think the passengers dealt with such terrible and challenging conditions? Share your thoughts.

Discussion Question

Tensions among the colonists surfaced even before they disembarked the Mayflower because it had landed in Massachusetts instead of Virginia. Those not part of the congregation claimed the contract with the Virginia Company was null and void. They believed they were free of the charter's jurisdiction because the Mayflower had landed in disputed waters. What would you do in this situation? Discuss.

Discussion Question

An initial group of passengers had been sent out from the Mayflower in aid of exploring the new territory in search of any dangers or potential problems. Their small shallop had been damaged on the voyage, so the passengers went to the beach on foot to collect firewood and take long-awaited (albeit rather chilly) baths in the ocean. The colonists relied heavily on the Mayflower as a floating home for the first few months. What potential dangers do you think they were keeping an eye out for? Discuss.

Discussion Question

The Pilgrims believed in their journey, and this belief is, without a doubt, something to admire. Yet, like the story of all explorers of the new world, it is more complicated than it appears. When the Pilgrims arrived on the shores of America, it was already occupied by the native people who saw the land as their own and had established roots there. Yet, as is the case around the world, the Pilgrims and the Native Americans tried to live together, but in the end, peace was overthrown by bloodshed. Do you think colonization could have been avoided? Why or why not? Share your thoughts.

ChapterTwelve
Quiz Question

1. **True/False:**In 1544 King Henry VIII, England's reigning monarch, broke away from the Roman Catholic Church. He then established the Church of England, to which he was the head, not the Catholic Pope. In doing this, King Henry set about changing the world as people knew it, including the lives of the Pilgrims.

2. **True/False:**It was two Puritan leaders, John Carver and Robert Cushman, who traveled to England to acquire a land patent which they could acquire in June 1619. According to billofrightsinstitute.org, "after much diligence, the congregation eventually secured a patent in 1619 from the Virginia Company, a private joint-stock venture which technically owned the land in North America. This patent would allow them to settle in North America while retaining a sense of their English identity.

3. **True/False:**The decision to immigrate to a country like America was fraught with uncertainty at the time due to reports of failed colonies. There were worries that the locals would be hostile, that there wouldn't be any food or water, that they may come into contact with unidentified diseases, and that traveling by sea was always dangerous. However, they felt pressured for a time as the truce that had been struck after the Ninety Years' War was in jeopardy, and there was anxiety among the congregation at how this might again change the tides in Europe.

4. **True/False:**On 6 November 1620, the Mayflower finally caught its first glimpse of the New World. However, what they saw was not the Hudson River; rather, they realized that their route had left them much farther north, off the Cape Cod coast. This was where their real challenge started. They were left with nothing but their wits and their supplies to keep them alive when they found themselves off the coast of an uncharted and frigid shoreline.

5. **True/ False:**In March of 1621, they had negotiated a pact of mutual protection with Ousamequin, chief of the neighboring Pokanoket Wampanoag tribe (also known as Massasoit to the

Pilgrims). There were six stipulations to the agreement. No one would do anything to hurt the other. Everything that was stolen would be given back, and the thief would be sent back to his own people to face justice. When the two groups got together, they made a pact to leave their weapons behind and work together as allies during battle.

6. **True/False:**The first American Thanksgiving was celebrated between the Pilgrims and a tribe of Native Americans known as the Wampanoag. There are several accounts of what occurred. According to history.com, the first American thanksgiving holiday "dates back to November 1621, when the newly arrived Pilgrims and the Wampanoag Indians gathered at Plymouth for an autumn harvest celebration."

7. **True/False:**The first missionaries to visit the Wampanoag area landed in 1632. A woman named John Eliot traveled all the way from Cambridge, England, in an effort to convert the Wampanoag to Christianity by translating the Bible and other Christian texts into Wopanaak (the Wampanoag language).

8. **True/ False:**Plymouth Colony had established a secure lifestyle by 1627. The harvests were plentiful, and families

expanded. Plymouth Colony had a population of roughly 160 in 1627.

Quiz Answer

1. False: It was 1534.

2. True

3. False: That event was the Eighty Years' War

4. True

5. True

6. True

7. False: John Eliot was a man

8. True

Bibliography

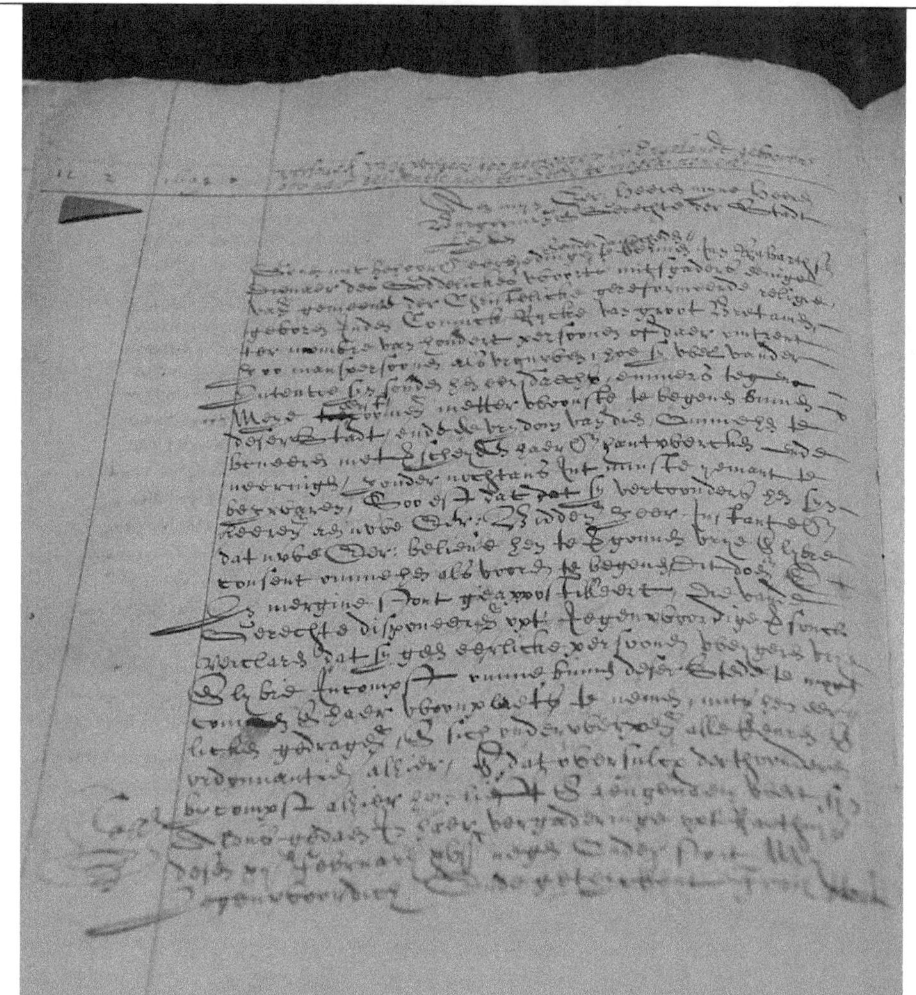

A letter of permission allowed the Pilgrims to settle in Holland.

The Puritans arrived in Holland filled with hope that this could become their new homeland. They wanted it to be a place where they could practice religious freedom in peace and out from under the oppressive thumb of the New Church of England. Yet they struggled to settle there, finding it very different from what they were used to in England.

The Puritan

According to plimoth.org, "a few people felt that the new Church retained too many practices of the Roman Church. They called for a return to a simpler faith and less structured forms of worship. In short, they wanted to return to worship in the way the early Christians had. Because these people

Aboard the Mayflower

On 6 September 1620, they finally sailed out for sea once

more, packing the Mayflower with as many passengers and

supplies as they dared. The crew and passengers sighed with

relief to finally be on their way and yet they had a long

journey ahead of them, one that would test their faith,

Plymouth Rock

The Mayflower eventually settled in what would become

known as Plymouth Harbor on the western side of Cape Cod

Bay in the middle of December. **(Wikipedia)**

Arriving in the New World

On 6 November 1620, the Mayflower finally caught their first glimpse of the New World. However, what they saw was not the Hudson River; rather, they realized that their route had left them much farther north, off the Cape Cod coast. This was where their real challenge started. They were left with nothing but their wits and their supplies to keep them alive when they found themselves off the coast of an uncharted and frigid shoreline. (worldhistory.org)

The First Thanksgiving

The first American Thanksgiving was celebrated between the

Pilgrims and a tribe of Native Americans known as the

Wampanoag. There are several accounts of what occurred.

According to history.com, the first American thanksgiving

holiday "dates back to November 1621, when the newly

arrived Pilgrims and the Wampanoag Indians gathered at

Plymouth for an autumn harvest celebration." (**History.com**)

The Thanksgiving Tradition

Whether they had turkey for their thanksgiving feast is debatable. In On Plymouth Plantation, Bradford noted that the colonists had a bountiful fall harvest because "there was a great store of wild turkeys, of which they took many, besides venison." Indeed, both English settlers and Native Americans relied heavily on wild turkey (but not domesticated turkey) as a food supply. Nonetheless, it is also possible that the hunters brought back other birds like ducks, geese, and swans, which we know the colonists ate on a regular basis. Herbs, onions, or

nuts might have been used to enhance the flavor of the birds

in place of bread stuffing. (Wikipedia)

Bonus Downloads

*Get Free Books with **Any Purchase** History Hub*

Every purchase comes with a FREE download!

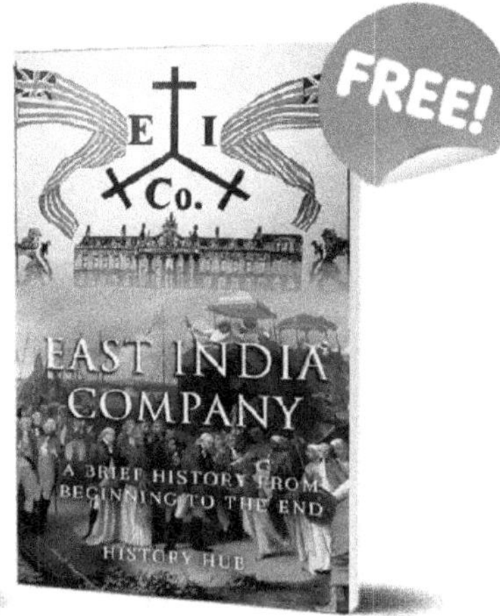

Thank You For Reading

As an independent publisher

with a tiny marketing budget

we rely on readers, like you.

If you're receiving help from this book,

would you please take a moment to write a brief review?

We really appreciate it.